PRAISE & WORSHIP DUETS

CONTENTS

— PIANO LEVEL —
LATE INTERMEDIATE/EARLY ADVANCED

ISBN 978-0-634-09323-4

7777 W. BLUEMOUND RD. P.O. BOX 13819 MILWAUKEE, WI 53213

Visit Hal Leonard Online at
www.halleonard.com

Visit Phillip at
www.phillipkeveren.com

AS THE DEER

Words and Music by MARTIN NYSTROM
Arranged by Phillip Keveren

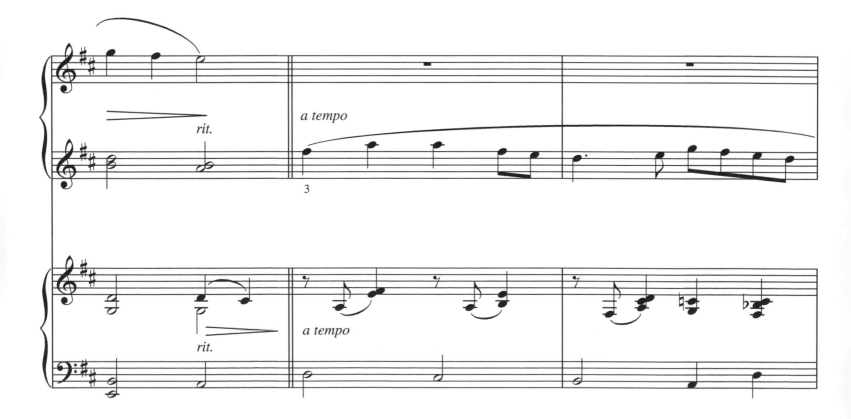

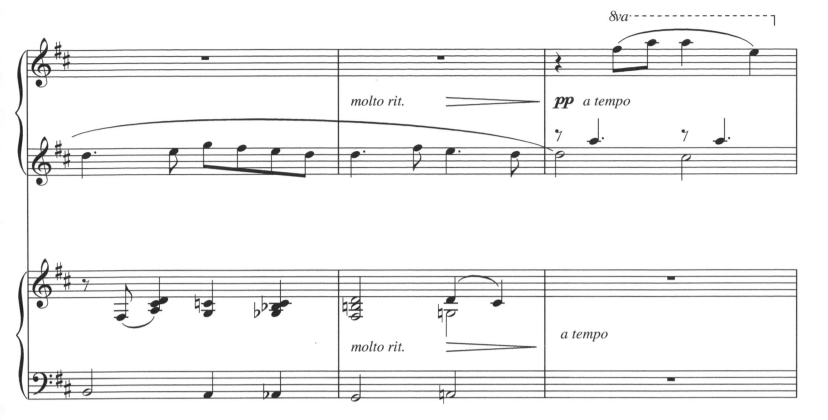

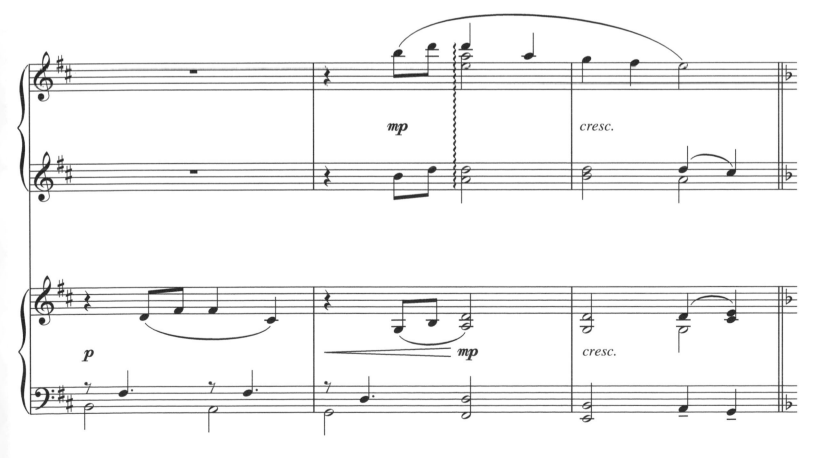

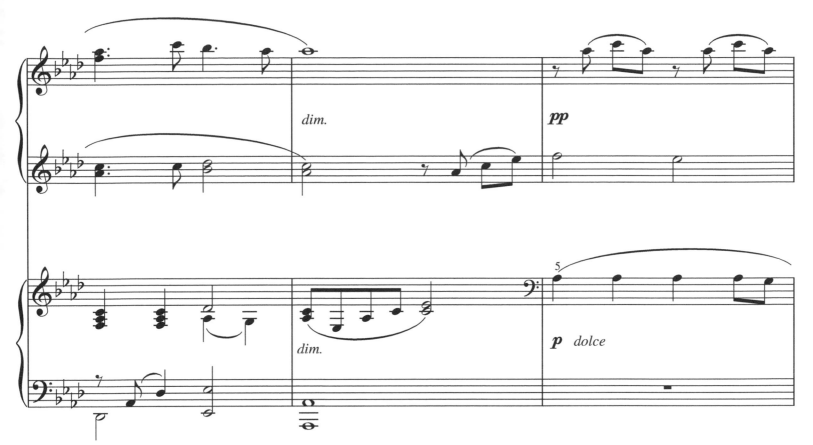

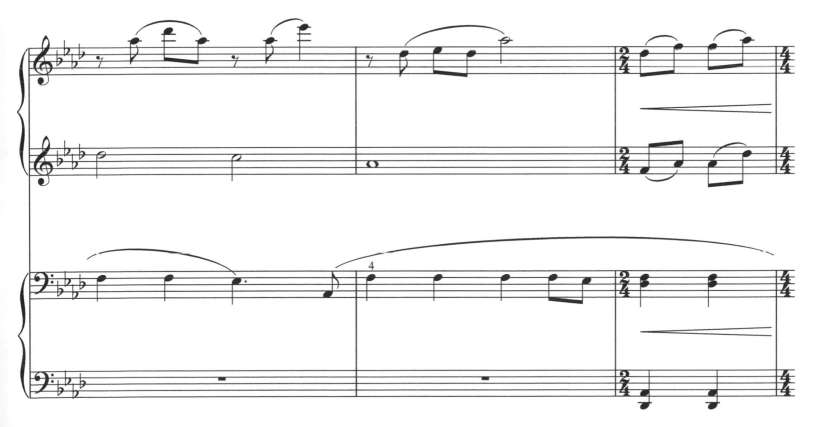

Majestically

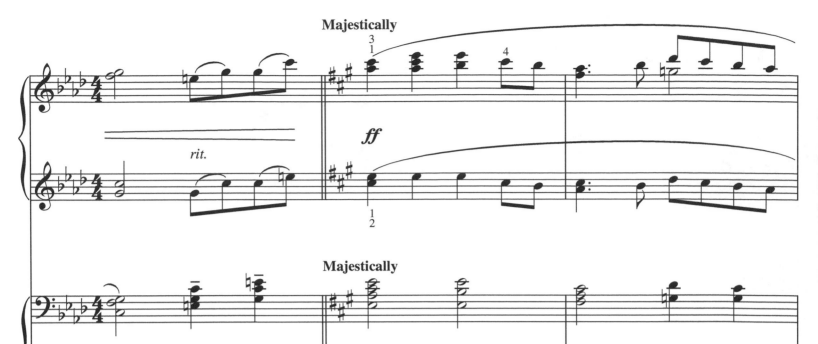

Majestically

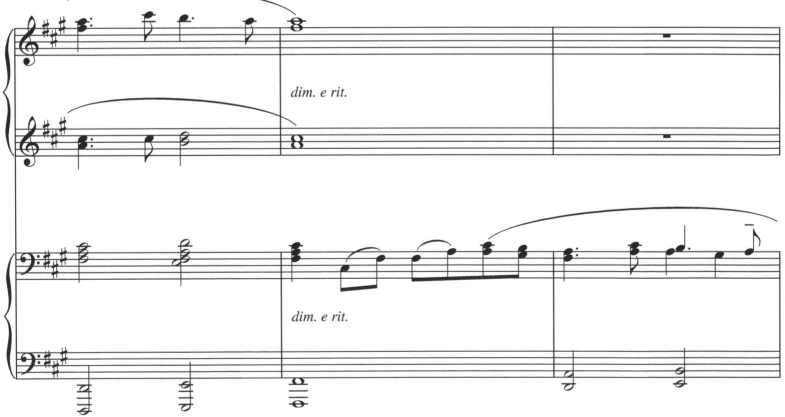

AWESOME GOD

Words and Music by RICH MULLINS
Arranged by Phillip Keveren

Slightly faster

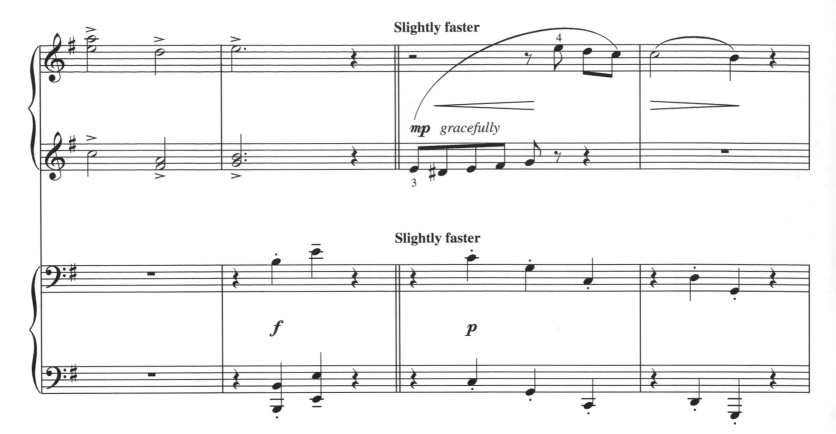

Slightly faster

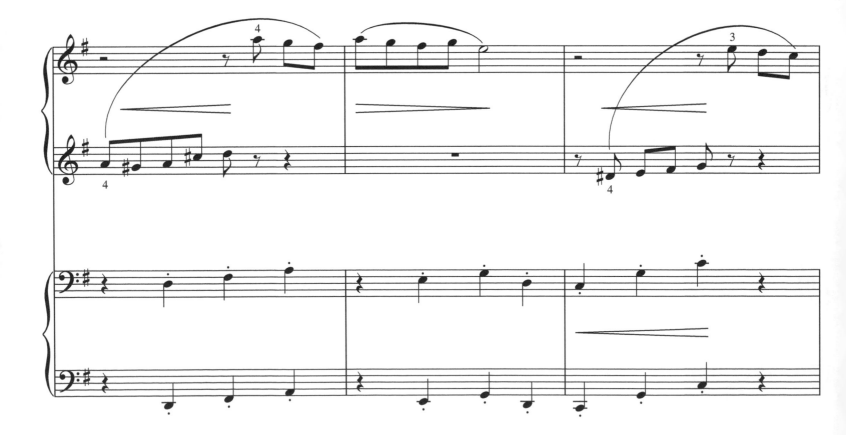

GIVE THANKS

Words and Music by HENRY SMITH
Arranged by Phillip Keveren

D.S. al Coda

CODA

GREAT IS THE LORD

Words and Music by MICHAEL W. SMITH
and DEBORAH D. SMITH
Arranged by Phillip Keveren

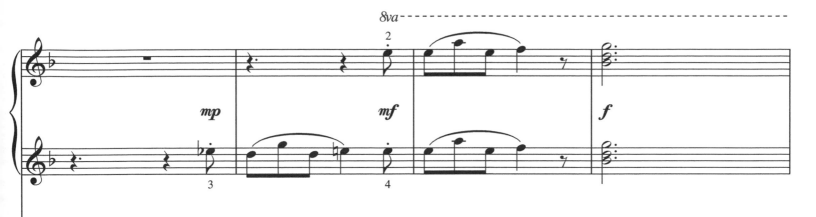

LORD, I LIFT YOUR NAME ON HIGH

Words and Music by RICK FOUNDS
Arranged by Phillip Keveren

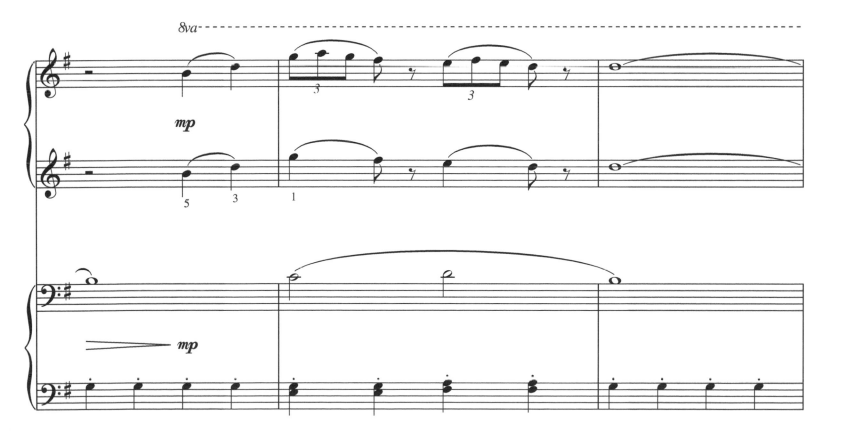

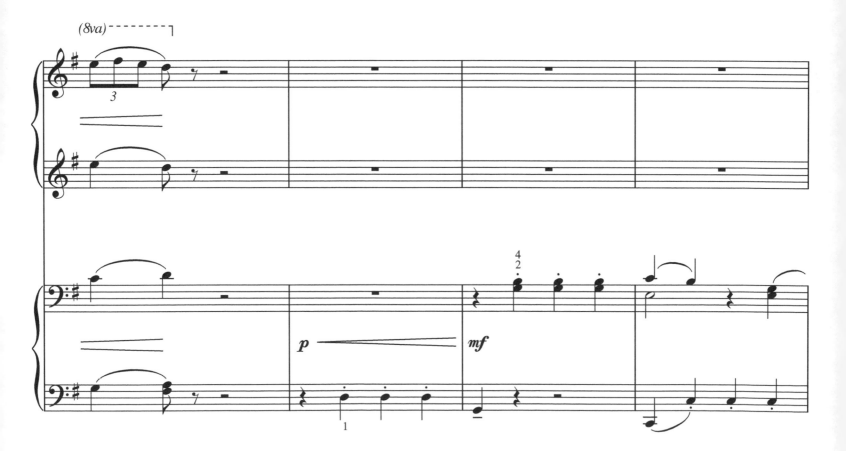

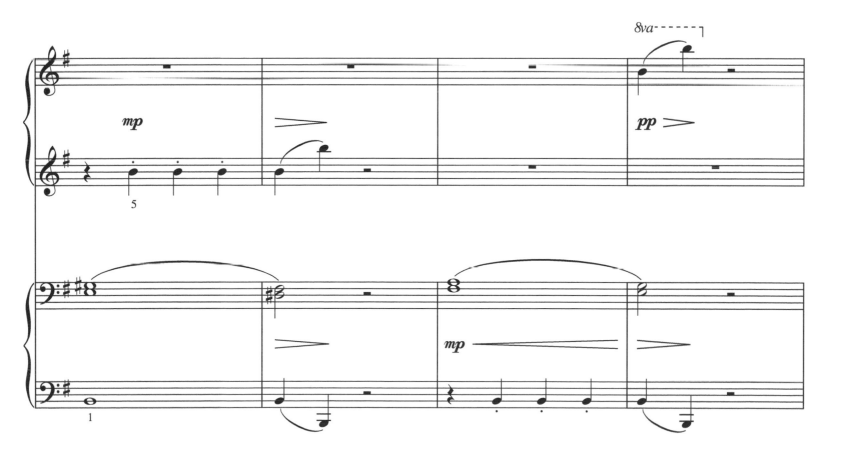

Brightly (in one)

Brightly (in one)

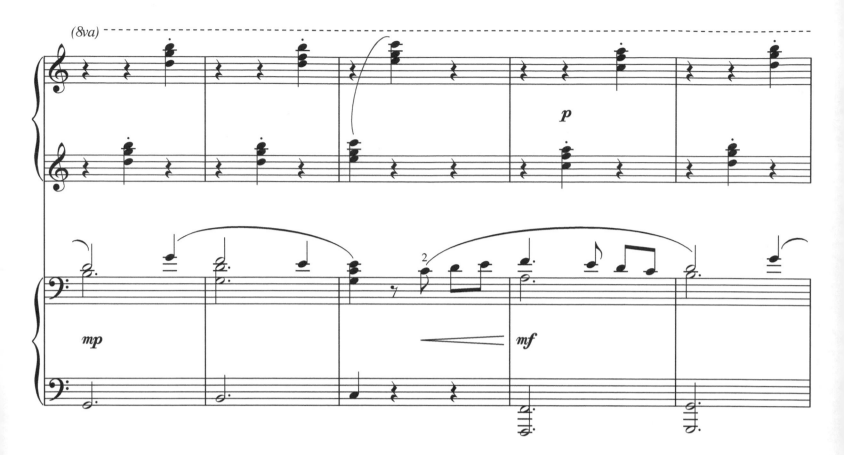

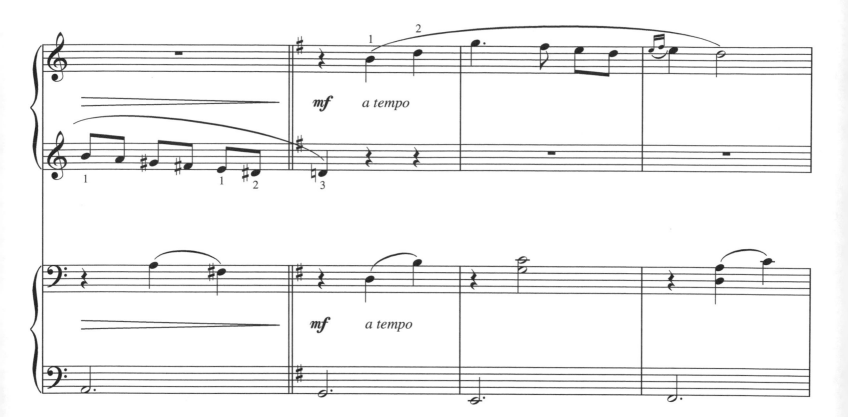

SHOUT TO THE LORD

Words and Music by DARLENE ZSCHECH
Arranged by Phillip Keveren

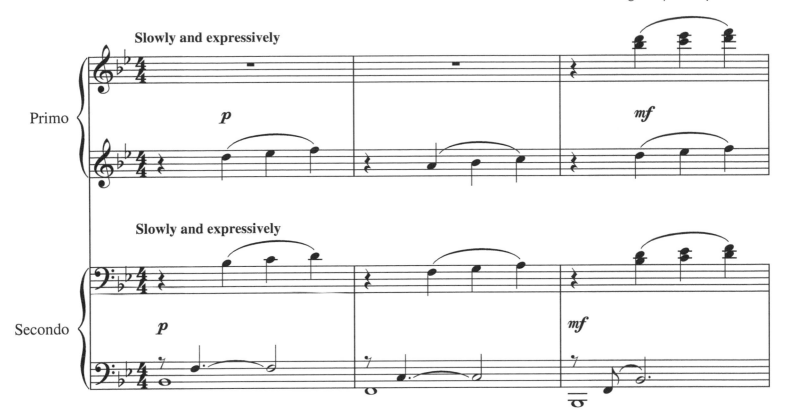

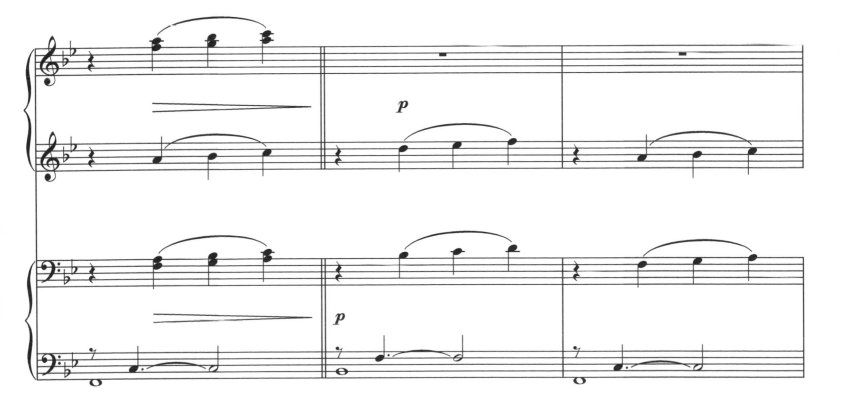

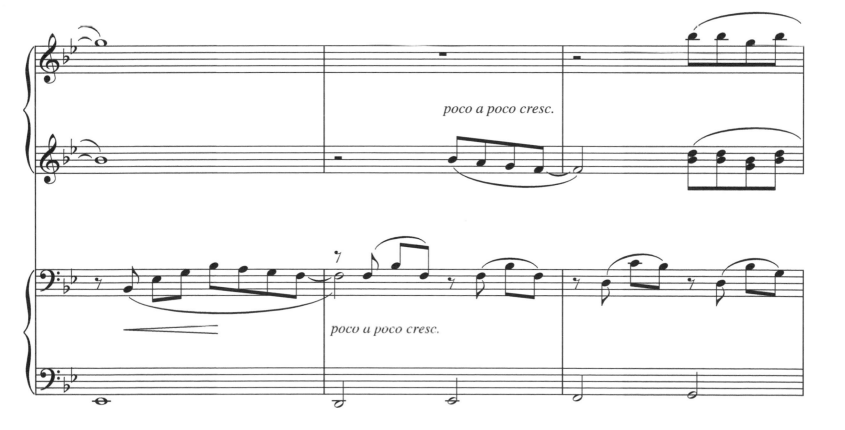

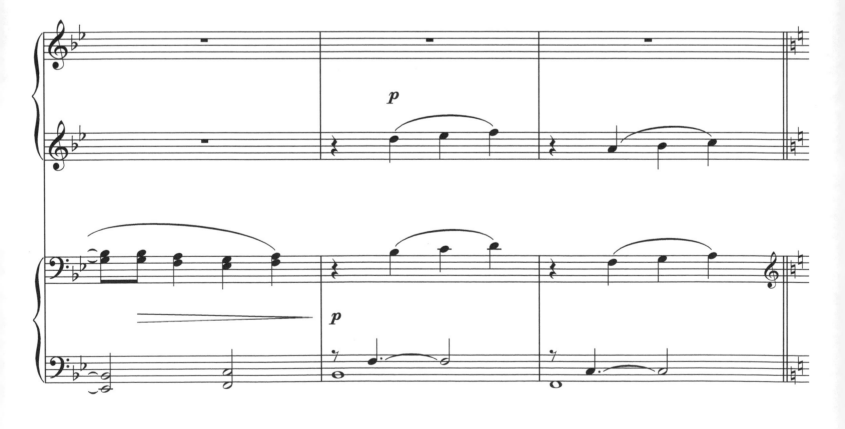

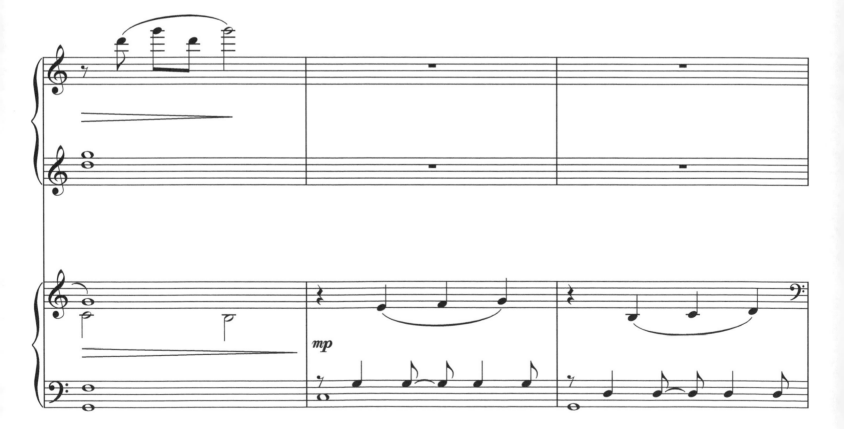

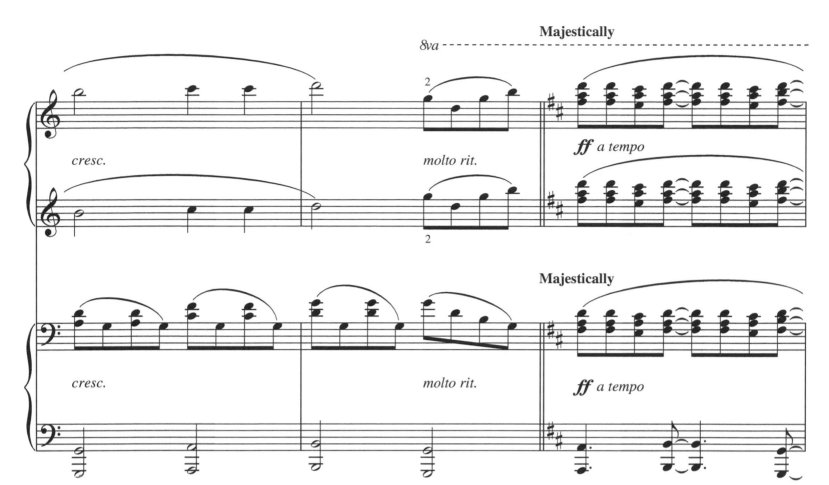

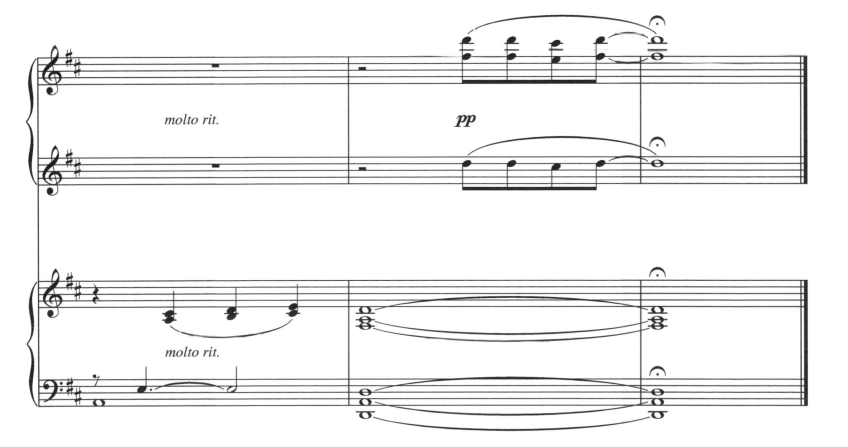

THERE IS A REDEEMER

Words and Music by MELODY GREEN
Arranged by Phillip Keveren

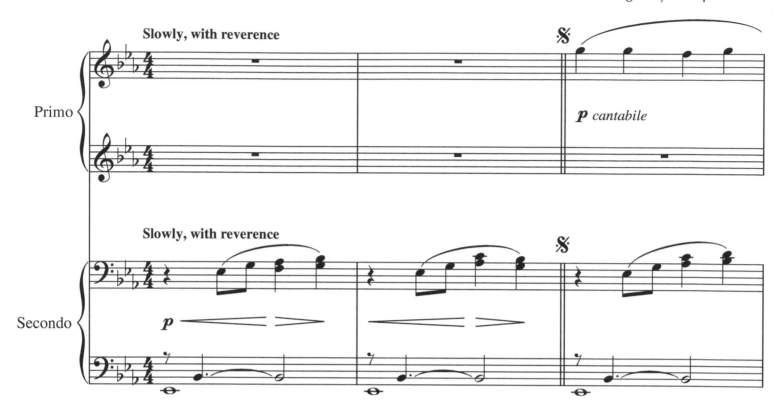

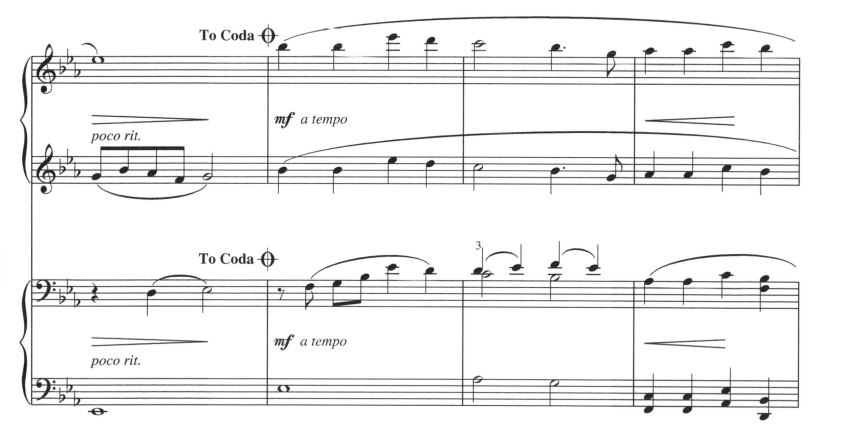

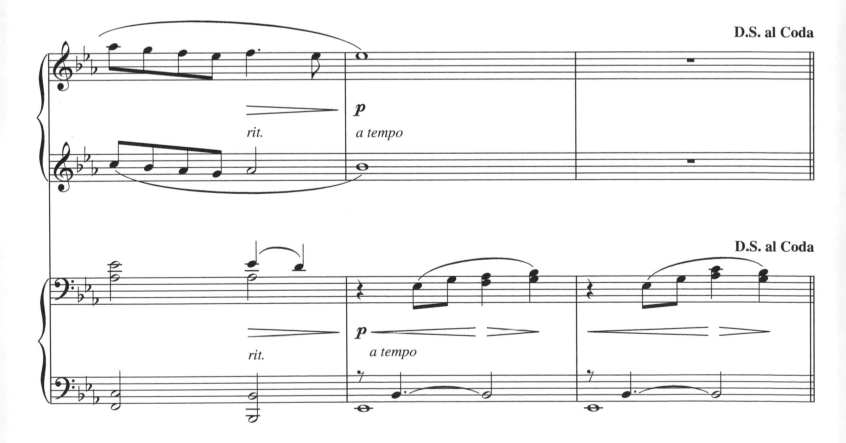

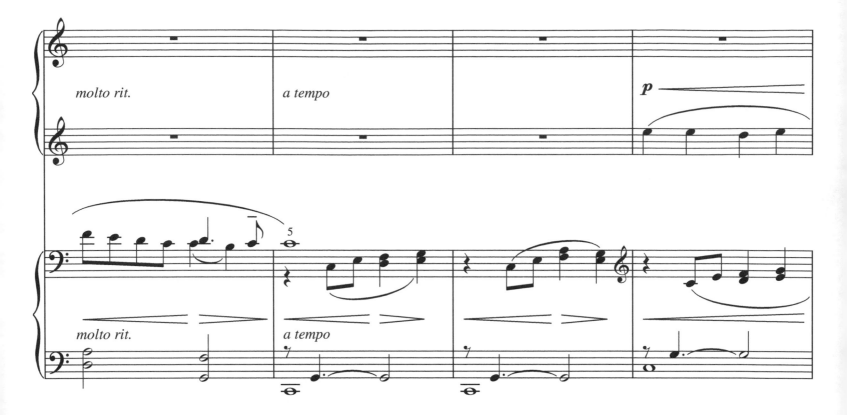

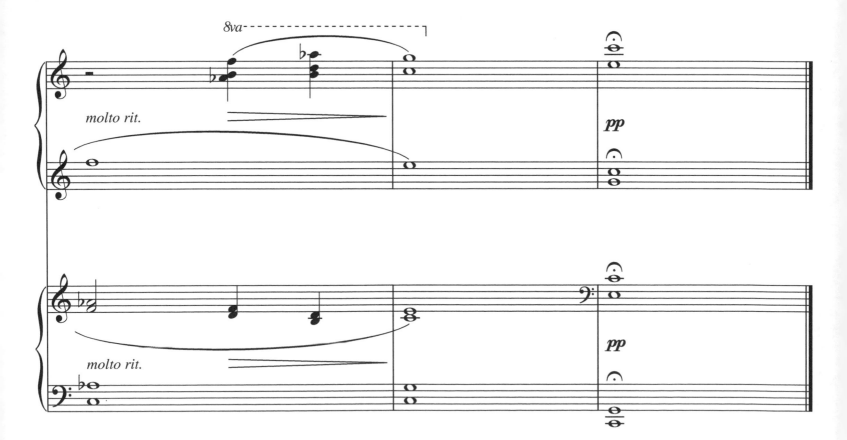

WE FALL DOWN

Words and Music by CHRIS TOMLIN
Arranged by Phillip Keveren

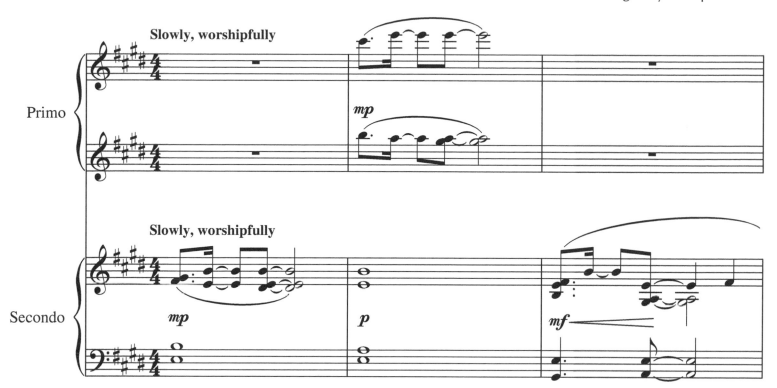

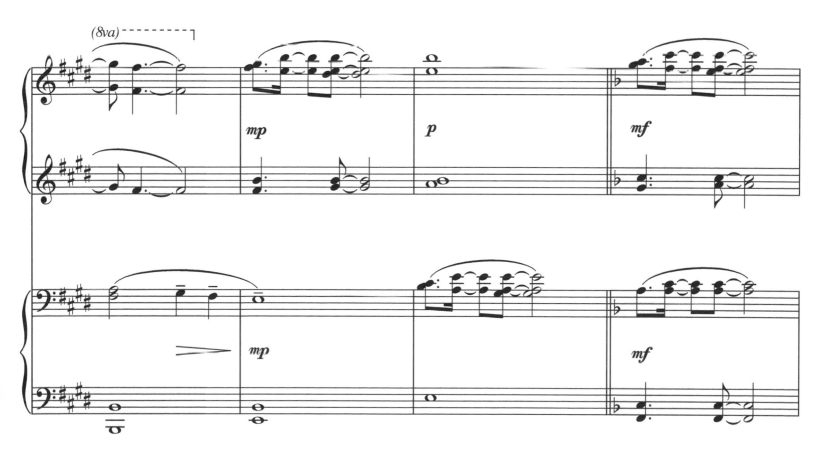

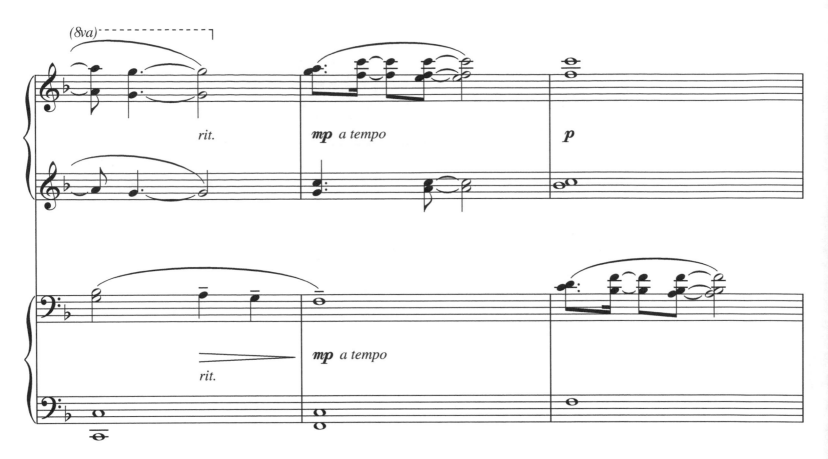